All Families

Two-Mom Families

by Connor Stratton

www.focusreaders.com

Copyright © 2025 by Focus Readers®, Mendota Heights, MN 55120. All rights reserved. No part of this book may be reproduced or utilized in any form or by any means without written permission from the publisher.

Focus Readers is distributed by North Star Editions:
sales@northstareditions.com | 888-417-0195

Produced for Focus Readers by Red Line Editorial.

Photographs ©: Shutterstock Images, cover, 1, 7, 8, 11, 16, 21, 29; iStockphoto, 4, 13, 14–15, 19, 22, 25, 27

Library of Congress Cataloging-in-Publication Data
Names: Stratton, Connor, author.
Title: Two-mom families / by Connor Stratton.
Description: Mendota Heights, MN: Focus Readers, [2025] | Series: All families | Includes index. | Audience: Grades 2-3
Identifiers: LCCN 2024036472 (print) | LCCN 2024036473 (ebook) | ISBN 9798889983958 (hardcover) | ISBN 9798889984238 (paperback) | ISBN 9798889984788 (pdf) | ISBN 9798889984511 (ebook)
Subjects: LCSH: Families--Juvenile literature. | Gay-parent families--Juvenile literature. | Mother and child--Juvenile literature.
Classification: LCC HQ755.85 .S768 2025 (print) | LCC HQ755.85 (ebook) | DDC 306.85086/643--dc23/eng/20240911
LC record available at https://lccn.loc.gov/2024036472
LC ebook record available at https://lccn.loc.gov/2024036473

Printed in the United States of America
Mankato, MN
012025

About the Author

Connor Stratton writes and edits nonfiction children's books. He lives in Minnesota.

Table of Contents

CHAPTER 1
Mother's Day 5

CHAPTER 2
About Two-Mom Families 9

 MANY IDENTITIES
The LGBTQ+ Community 14

CHAPTER 3
Similarities and Challenges 17

CHAPTER 4
Questions and Strengths 23

Focus on Two-Mom Families • 28
Glossary • 30
To Learn More • 31
Index • 32

Chapter 1

Mother's Day

A boy wakes up excited. Today is Mother's Day. First, he runs out to the backyard. He picks a tulip. One of his moms loves flowers. Then, the boy runs into the kitchen. He gets a delicious bar of chocolate.

Flowers and food are common Mother's Day gifts. So are cards.

His other mom doesn't care about flowers. But she loves chocolate.

Next, the boy gets two pieces of paper. He makes Mother's Day cards for both of his moms. He tapes the tulip to one card. He tapes the chocolate to the other. The boy gives the cards to his moms. They give him a loving hug.

Did You Know?

In the United States, Mother's Day falls on the second Sunday of May.

 People write Mother's Day cards to say what they love about their moms.

Later, the family sits on the couch. The boy's siblings join. The moms tell them the story of how their family formed. The boy asks lots of questions. His moms give good answers. The boy feels lucky to be part of such a great family.

Chapter 2

About Two-Mom Families

Many families have two moms. These families start with two women who love each other. They want to care for a child. The family can form in different ways.

 In the early 2020s, about one in five female couples had children.

Sometimes, families use **IVF**. A **donor** helps begin this process. Then, one mom gets pregnant with the help of a doctor. She might use an egg from her own body. Or, the other mom might donate her egg. Next, the pregnant mom gives birth to the baby. Both moms raise the child together.

Other two-mom families are adoptive. Adoptive families involve different birth parents. The birth parents were not able to raise the

 Millions of children have been born through IVF.

child. They wanted the child to be cared for. So, they let other parents adopt the child.

A two-mom family might also involve an earlier relationship. A mom had a partner in the past. The two had children. They became the birth parents. At some point, the adults' relationship ended. Then the mom began a new relationship. In the new relationship, the two moms raise the children. The other birth

Did You Know?

LGBTQ+ parents adopt more often than other parents.

 Some LGBTQ+ families include stepparents and stepchildren.

parent might still be part of the family. When that happens, it's a blended family.

MANY IDENTITIES

The LGBTQ+ Community

Each letter in LGBTQ+ stands for something. They mean **lesbian**, gay, bisexual, trans, and **queer**. The plus sign stands for the many other **sexualities** and genders.

Many mothers in two-mom families **identify** as lesbian or gay. They are **attracted** to people of the same gender. Some moms are bisexual. They are attracted to their same gender. And they're also attracted to others. Some moms are trans. A trans person's gender is different from what doctors or other adults assigned them at birth. Many moms identify as queer, too.

About one in ten LGBTQ+ parents are transgender moms.

Chapter 3

Similarities and Challenges

In many ways, two-mom families are similar to other kinds of families. For example, kids in two-mom families grow up with loving parents. Two-mom families also care for their community.

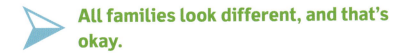 All families look different, and that's okay.

They visit with friends. They see extended family members, too.

However, some people believe unfair things about the LGBTQ+ community. They think kids need one mom and one dad. These beliefs are not true. All kinds of

Did You Know?

People in adoptive families may look different from one another. They might not look like their parents. Kids sometimes get questions or strange looks. That can feel upsetting.

 Researchers have shown that kids in two-mom families are just as healthy as other kids.

adults make loving parents. And people can love whoever they want to.

Some people act on their unfair beliefs. They mistreat LGBTQ+ people. This is discrimination.

Some discrimination has to do with sexuality. That is called **homophobia**. Some mistreatment is because of gender. That is often **transphobia**.

Sometimes kids experience discrimination. A classmate might say something harmful. Kids might be teased about not having a dad. They may also see people mistreat their moms.

Mistreatment is painful. Kids may feel angry or upset. They may feel

 Kids can speak to counselors if they experience bullying.

confused. They might have many feelings at once. All these feelings are okay. It can help to talk about them with a trusted adult. Kids can find different ways to work through their feelings.

Chapter 4

Questions and Strengths

Kids in two-mom families might have questions. They may want to know how their families formed. Kids might want to know about their birth parents. Or they may want to learn about the donor.

 Kids should be honest about their feelings, and parents should be honest when answering questions.

It can be important to talk openly about these stories.

Sometimes, it's possible to meet these people. Kids may want to meet donors or birth parents. If they do, that can also be helpful.

Kids can be proud to be part of their two-mom family. These families have many strengths.

Did You Know?

In 2015, the United States began allowing same-sex marriage.

 Some kids want to meet donors or birth parents, and others don't. Both choices are okay.

Being different can help people be more open. They understand that families come in all types.

They may feel more comfortable with people who aren't like them.

Another strength comes from the moms. These parents are **resilient**. They live in a world that doesn't always understand them. Even so, they chose to be themselves. That is brave. The two moms can help kids be resilient, too.

Belonging to the LGBTQ+ community is also a strength. Kids are part of a larger group. That can help kids be more accepting of

 Many people in the LGBTQ+ community celebrate at Pride parades.

themselves. They may feel free to explore their own identities. As they do, kids will have a big community to support them.

FOCUS ON
Two-Mom Families

Write your answers on a separate piece of paper.

1. Summarize the main ideas of Chapter 4.

2. What are some things about your family that make you feel proud? Why?

3. What does the G in LGBTQ+ stand for?
    - A. gay
    - B. great
    - C. group

4. How are mothers in two-mom families resilient?
    - A. They are strong enough to raise a family in a world that doesn't always understand them.
    - B. They raise their family to always be the same as everyone else.
    - C. They raise a family that avoids talking about complicated feelings.

5. What does **assigned** mean in this book?

*Some moms are trans. A trans person's gender is different from what doctors or other adults **assigned** them at birth.*

   A. avoided
   B. changed
   C. selected

6. What does **blended family** mean in this book?

*In the new relationship, the two moms raise the children. The other birth parent might still be part of the family. When that happens, it's a **blended family**.*

   A. families with kids from earlier relationships
   B. families without any kids
   C. families that look similar

Answer key on page 32.

Glossary

attracted
Pulled toward someone in a close or loving way.

donor
A person who gives something in order to help others.

homophobia
Hatred or mistreatment of people because of their sexuality.

identify
To define oneself in a certain way.

IVF
A medical process to help adults have babies.

lesbian
Having to do with attraction between women.

queer
Identifying with a gender or sexuality that is different from what society thinks is normal.

resilient
Able to heal and become stronger after a hard time.

sexualities
Identities that describe who people are attracted to.

transphobia
Hatred or mistreatment of people because their gender is different from what they were assigned at birth.

To Learn More

BOOKS

Johnson, Chelsea, LaToya Council, and Carolyn Choi. *Love Without Bounds: An IntersectionAllies Book About Families*. New York: Dottir Press, 2023.

Lombardo, Jennifer. *The Story of the LGBTQ+ Rights Movement*. Buffalo, NY: Cavendish Square Publishing, 2024.

Prager, Sarah. *A Child's Introduction to Pride: The Inspirational History and Culture of the LGBTQIA+ Community*. New York: Black Dog & Leventhal, 2023.

NOTE TO EDUCATORS

Visit **www.focusreaders.com** to find lesson plans, activities, links, and other resources related to this title.

Index

A
adoptive families, 10–11, 12, 18

B
birth parents, 10–12, 23–24
blended family, 12–13

C
communication, 21, 23–24

D
discrimination, 19–20
donor, 10, 23–24

E
extended family, 18

H
homophobia, 20

I
identities, 14, 27

L
LGBTQ+ community, 12, 14, 18–19, 26

R
resilient, 26

S
sexualities, 14, 20

T
transphobia, 20

Answer Key: **1.** Answers will vary; **2.** Answers will vary; **3.** A; **4.** A; **5.** C; **6.** A